Sammy
Hero At Age Five

M. Schmidt

Gene D. Donley

Fresh Ink Group
Guntersville

Sammy:
Hero At Age Five

Copyright © 2018
by M. Schmidt and Gene D. Donley
M. Schmidt Productions
All rights reserved

Fresh Ink Group
An Imprint of:
The Fresh Ink Group, LLC
Box 931
Guntersville, AL 35976
Email: info@FreshInkGroup.com
FreshInkGroup.com

Edition 1.0   2018

All photos © S. Donley, G. Donley, & M. Schmidt
Book design by Amit Dey / FIG
Interior photo design M. Schmidt / MSP
Cover art by Anik / FIG
Cover by Geez / FIG

This narrative is based on a true story using journals and notes belonging to the authors, and from the point of view of Sammy, as noted by his mom and big brother. The reader will read this memoir through the eyes and soul of a five-year-old boy with cancer. Except as permitted under the U.S. Copyright Act of 1976, no part of this publication may be reproduced, distributed, or transmitted in any form or by any means, or stored in a database or retrieval system, without prior written permission of the Fresh Ink Group, LLC. Except for brief quotations in critical reviews or articles, no portion of this book's copyrighted content may be stored in any medium, transmitted in any form, used in whole or part, or sourced for derivative works such as videos, television, and motion pictures, without prior written permission from the authors. The authors wish to thank all the caring physicians, nurses, and social workers involved with Sam's care; and those who remained a constant in Gene's life.

BISAC Subject Headings:
BIO026000 **BIOGRAPHY & AUTOBIOGRAPHY** / Personal Memoirs
JNF049180 **JUVENILE NONFICTION** /
Religious / Christian / Biography & Autobiography
JNF024020 **JUVENILE NONFICTION** /
Health & Daily Living / Diseases, Illnesses & Injuries

Library of Congress Control Number: 2018912298

ISBN-13: 978-1-947867-29-1 Papercover
ISBN-13: 978-1-947867-30-7 Hardcover
ISBN-13: 978-1-947867-31-4 Ebooks

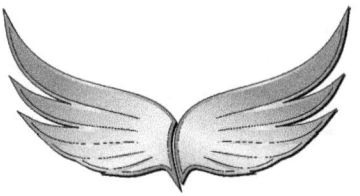

Dedication

Always to brothers Shane and Gene. We both love you, Gene.
Nice to see you in Heaven, Shane, Ardy, Dale, and Slim.
And to Mom, for being there for me.

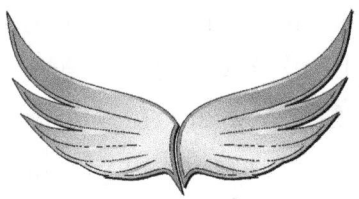

Reviews

Sammy: Hero at Age Five had me hooked from page one, and I found myself trying to put my own person into the shoes of a five year old boy who became a hero. Actually, he was a hero since his conception, and the title is highly fitting. This story is a memoir, a child's memoir—and Christian, written by his mother and big brother, using elements of Sammy's short life on Earth. I laughed at the early years and found myself sad in places. This is a truly heartwarming story filled with precious memories and the presence of Jesus. I don't want to give away anything but I will say this is a fast read, funny, sad, real life and heartwarming. The photographs included throughout complete this five star read.

~ Jana N., Reader

I wasn't sure what I was going to actually read when I agreed to be a beta reader. I must say that I am forever changed since reading, *Sammy: Hero at Age Five*. Written from the point of view of a five year old little boy, this book and all that happens both funny and sad are moments that all children fighting cancer, their siblings, and their parents should read. The antics of Sam and his big brother, Gene, are funny and scary at times, but they are real—real-life events and situations. Jesus was evident throughout this short story and I found the photographs to be endearing as I read along. All children who suffer from cancer and their families could benefit from, and relate to, this short story. Highly recommended and five stars all the way.

~ Susan Vance, Author of *Forever My Sister*

This book deserves five stars. It is well written and will keep you captivated right along with Sammy as he unfolds his story about a horrific battle with cancer and the other issues that came along with healing. *Sammy: Hero at Age Five* is definitely an emotional roller coaster. To say I loved this story would be an untruth because I didn't like reading what happened to this sweet little boy and his family. What I did love, was the way the authors portrayed Sammy's attitude throughout his battles. Sammy was a feisty little thing with a huge heart and desire to achieve his goals, and his relationship with Jesus was incredible for someone so little. I highly recommend this book to families facing such trials. I know they would gather courage and inspiration along with an appreciation of life on earth and what awaits them in heaven with Jesus by reading Sammy's story."

~ Raven H. Price, Author of *Wisdom's Song*

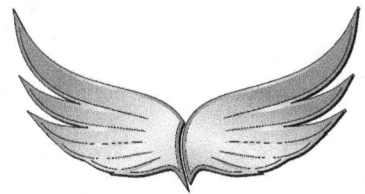

Table of Contents

Prologue xi

PART ONE: I Was Born 1
Chapter One 3
Chapter Two 7
Chapter Three 10
Chapter Four 13
Chapter Five 17
Chapter Six 20

PART TWO: Cancer Arrived 23
Chapter Seven 25
Chapter Eight 28
Chapter Nine 32
Chapter Ten 40
Chapter Eleven 44

Chapter Twelve. 47
Chapter Thirteen 56
Chapter Fourteen 64
Chapter Fifteen. 72
About the Authors 77

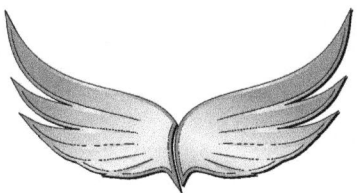

Prologue

I had cancer at age four, and I beat my cancer, too! Even though I passed away, I wanted to share with other children and family my thoughts during my cancer battle. My Mom kept detailed notes and my big brother, Gene, helped her. The timeline in my story changes as my thoughts and memories changed.

With that, I will now write a few memories of my short life sprinkled with some photos. I was always called Sammy until we learned of my cancer. At the big hospital, KUMC, the nurses started calling me Sam, and I have been Sam ever since.

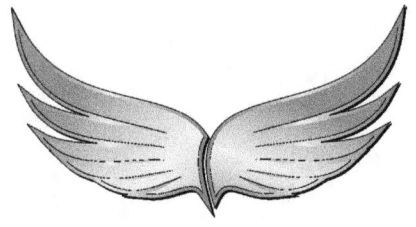

PART ONE:

I Was Born

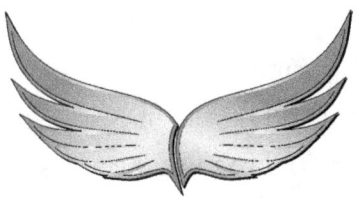

Chapter One

Mom told me that I was born the day before Easter in 1985. I don't remember myself as a baby or toddler, but in the pictures I have seen I smiled a lot. Mom also told me that I had an older brother named Shane, and that he died while still inside her tummy. I never understood how this could happen, and if I asked Mom she would start crying. As I grew up, and got a few months to my age, I realized that I had a big brother - Gene!

One Christmas Mom bought both of us red Big Wheels, and she put them together by herself, one at a time after we had gone to bed. Then she hid them in the laundry room until Christmas day.

I always looked up to my big brother. He was a year older, and he knew a lot more than I did. We would play chase or ride our red Big Wheels, and we could fight just as easy as we could play. Mom said we were "two peas in a pod," but I never understood what that meant. Mom took us to the park in town often, and she would pull us in a red wagon all the way there and back. We had crawdads. They had pincers and it was fun for Brother and me to figure out how to pick them up. Back then, we fished a lot in the Smoky Hill River, trying to catch catfish and white bass each spring.

Summers were hot and humid in Kansas, and some days it was hard to breathe. Mom told me I had exercise-induced asthma, and I really never understood what that meant as, I was just a little boy.

Gene and I were out in the east garage one summer day, and we found a huge bull snake! We went there to ride our Big Wheels around inside and in and out of the garage like we had done in the past. I was three and a half years old at the time.

Gene, Mom, and Sam in the Hospital and Sam is One Day Old

Mom was cooking dinner, and Gene went and told on me! He told her that I had cornered a snake in the garage. Mom ran out and found me riding closer and closer to a coiled, and ready to strike, king-sized bull snake. Our neighbor Slim heard the ruckus going on and he came over. Once he saw the snake, he took a shovel and killed it. Slim knew that the snake could hurt us, and he knew Brother or I might have an allergy to it. Slim was a smart man and all of us loved him.

I have lots of memories of Slim. For one, Mom always gave Brother and me a bath together as we were only ages three and four. She never trusted us in the bath by ourselves, and she gave us our baths right before bedtime. She washed our hair and rinsed it with fresh water. When it came time to get out of the bathtub, we were adamant that we would not get out and, as usual, Mom would grab one of us boys and help us dry off. Mom took turns each evening as who she would pluck out of the bathtub! Once dried off, both my brother and I would take off, and run stark naked through the kitchen and dining rooms, and into the living room. We would run naked around the sofa our father was always sitting on and the stuffed chair that Slim would be sitting in. It was only a matter of time until Mom caught us and made us put on our pajamas.

Slim was in our home three or four evenings a week, sometimes he ate dinner with us, and other times he only had dessert, usually homemade cherry, peach, or apple pie. He was like a grandpa to us boys, and we loved him. He didn't date, drink alcohol, or go out, as he preferred to be at our house or his families' homes in town. Slim grew a huge garden and gave us a lot of corn, onions, watermelons, cantaloupes, and whatever

Gene, Mom, & Sam 3 Days Old

else he grew. He always gave us a lot of fresh produce, and he also gave away fresh produce to other family and friends in our town of about 700 people. He loved to grow his garden each year. Mom planted a garden too, but it was tiny. We always had a lot of fresh tomatoes and cucumbers. Sometimes Gene would sneak into the little garden and find a radish. After yanking it out of the ground, he wiped it off and ate it! He did this with those small skinny onions, too. I never told Mom, but I think she knew anyway, as she always seemed to have eyes in the back of her head.

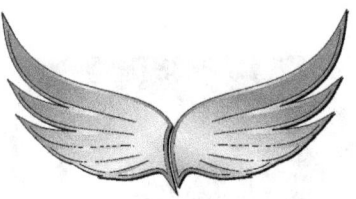

Chapter Two

My memories of Slim fill me with warmth and love, and it is nice to have him flying all angelic with Shane and me. Every chance we got we would sneak next door to Slim's, and Mom would always know as if she had eyes in the back of her head. In a way, she did, as she always simply knew things—something she inherited, probably. Mom always just knew things and she and Grandpa Copp were alike in that way.

We loved going into Slim's large garage. He had fishing boats and riding lawn mowers and more! We climbed onto and over everything, pretending to fish or mow, and we made sounds like engines. Sometimes, Mom would let us be here for a full 10 minutes before coming to get us. Even then, Mom and Slim would have a chat while we kept on playing.

I remember one Christmas when Slim gave my brother and me toy semi-trucks with storage inside of them. They were lots of fun to play with and we all had a great time.

On our second to last Christmas together on Earth, Mom bought us red bikes with training wheels, and Slim hid them in

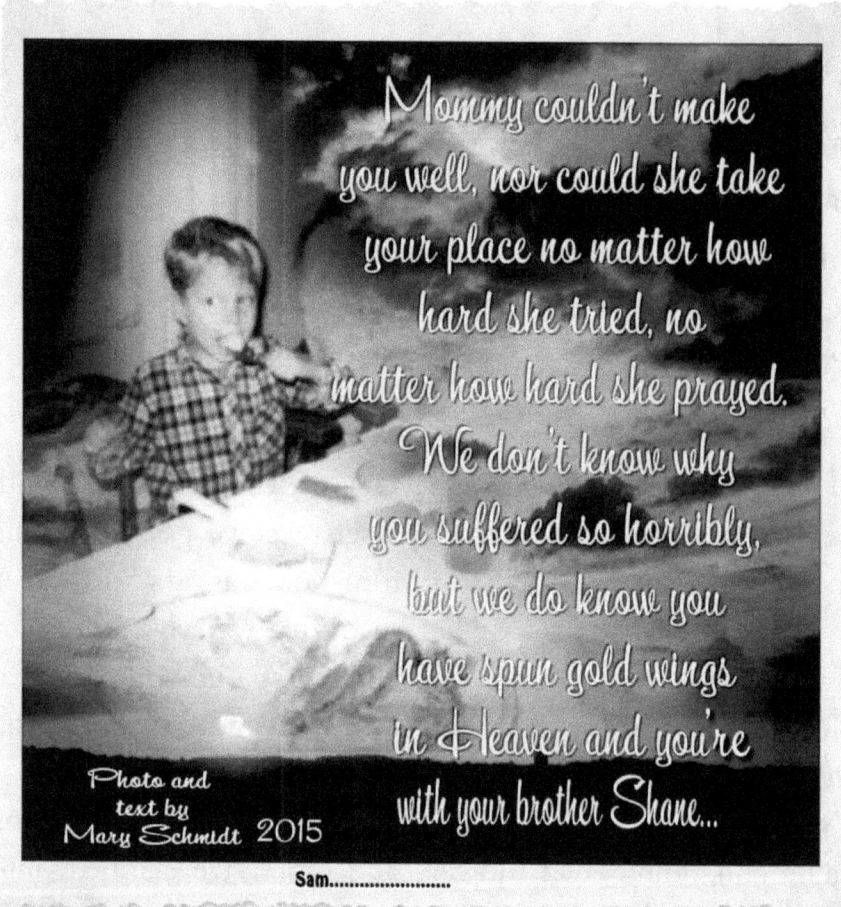

his garage until we were completely asleep on Christmas Eve. We woke up to find our bikes and we were determined to ride them inside the house since it was so cold outside. We did our best and it was fun!

Thanksgivings were always at our house, as we had a huge living room where everyone could visit. Sometimes I ate using my right hand, and other times I used my left hand. Mom called me "ambidextrous." I don't know what that meant, but she was

Chapter Two

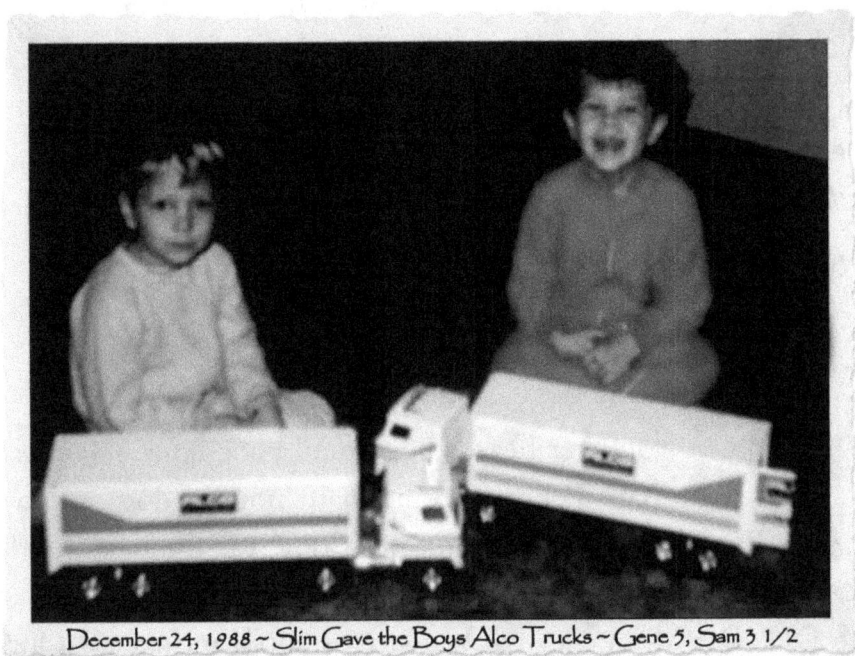

December 24, 1988 ~ Slim Gave the Boys Alco Trucks ~ Gene 5, Sam 3 1/2

happy about it, so I was as well. I loved the food! I loved the taste of all the great food! Meals and holidays are some of my favorite memories.

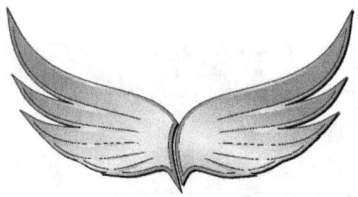

Chapter Three

Have you ever heard the name "Poochkins"? He was our half Pekingese and half poodle dog and we played with him a lot. That dog was the best buddy to my brother and me.

Did your Mom ever tell you stories about monsters? Ours did and often! You see, we lived in a house with a huge yard. I mean HUGE! At the north property line was a barbed wire fence and, of all things, our storm cellar filled with snakes. More on that storm cellar later.

Way beyond that fence line was a large old sand pit filled with water and all kinds of things that bite. Mom didn't want us to try to sneak off to that sand pit, so she made up a story about monsters living there and we stayed away from it! The only monster I knew was "Cookie Monster," who was a nice cuddly blue stuffed character we had, and loved.

After we got a little older, Mom would take us on hikes through parts of the sand pit. She pointed out the things that could bite, birds, poisonous plants, and the water. She said the monster lived in the water and that we couldn't ever go down there! That scared us! A year later my brother and I decided

April 6, 1988 ~ Sam's 3rd Birthday ~ Riding Big Wheels

to sneak off to the sand pit on our own—we didn't get far, as we became scared and ran back into our own yard. Mom was hanging out the wash on the clothesline, and she had kept an eye on us just to see how far we would get. Mom would have come after us if we hadn't run back on our own. We never went back - ever!

Now, about that storm cellar. Why would a person have a storm cellar located 200 yards from the house? I don't remember this but Brother does. I was about five months old and Gene was age two. A storm came upon us and we were inside the house. Gene and Mom said it sounded like a freight train it was so loud. Mom grabbed me in one arm, and Gene with her other hand, and she took us inside a closet and held both of us in her lap right next to the chimney. We had quilts over us and lost power. When the storm passed, we came out of the closet and saw half of our trees were down, shingles everywhere, and about two dozen boxcars had been tossed about. That tree-top tornado took off the top of the salt plant about two miles east of us and flipped semis over easily on Old 40 Hwy. Gene said he helped Mom with the cleanup and she agreed. I was too little to remember this happening and I'm okay with not remembering.

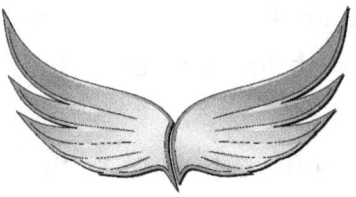

Chapter Four

One day Mom put up mini blinds on all of the windows in our huge living room. We helped out with handing her tools. The blinds were nice and she had better control in keeping the house cool in the summertime. Sometimes, Gene and I would try to pull the cords on the blinds as we watched Mom do this often. She would catch us and we would get a swat on our behinds, and then she placed the cords up higher and out of our reach.

I woke up early from my afternoon nap one day and I found Mom in the kitchen doing dishes, and she told me to get one of my toys and then come back into the kitchen. She had eyes in the back of her head! I know it and she saved my life. I decided to climb up on the top of an easy chair and pull a mini blind cord. Next thing I knew I was hanging with the cord around my neck, I couldn't breathe or yell for help, and BAM! Mom was there, she lifted me up, and removed the cord that was strangling me. I could finally breathe and that cord left a mark on my neck for a few days. We sat down on the sofa with me on her lap. Both of us were crying. Then Mom made me sit on the kitchen counter while she finished the dishes, the cords were placed higher up, and the furniture was moved, too. I scared Mom bad with this incident. Mom was shaking as she washed the dishes.

Gene would get into trouble too, and he would blame me for things. Mom knew better though. One day Mom was cooking bacon in the microwave oven. We loved bacon. Mom was helping me get my shoes tied when she smelled smoke, and she ran into the kitchen. The microwave was on fire! The cabinets started to burn. Mom yelled at Gene to leave the kitchen, and then she yanked on the refrigerator to unplug it and the microwave. Using soapy dishwater from the sink, she put out the fire. Gene had caused it. He had managed to open the

Sam 04 April 1988 ~ Age 3

Gene and Sam in Red Wagon Playing in Hall Entrance

microwave and tried to use a fork to get some bacon, but he wasn't tall enough to get any. When he couldn't get any bacon, he left the fork in the microwave and he hit buttons until it started to cook again. That caused the fire. Once the fire was out, Mom yelled at Gene and told him how bad it could have been. Then she simply held us to her sides on the couch for a while as we all calmed down. Mom cleaned up the mess later.

Gene did get me in trouble with him sometimes. Another day Mom went out to the garden to get some fresh tomatoes and we were told to stay inside, as she would be right back.

While we watched her, Gene messed with the doorknob and accidentally locked Mom out of the house. There she was, trying to convince us to unlock the door. Gene wasn't sure how to unlock it and we both were scared that we were in big trouble. Mom had to call for help, and finally a pickup truck with a ladder arrived. The man placed the ladder against the lower side of the house and removed a vent section that led into the attic. He was too big to get inside. Mom had to climb up and go through the vent opening. Mom doesn't like spiders and things, but she knew what she had to to do, so she stepped from wood two-by-four to wood two-by-four until she reached the chimney. Had Mom not stepped right, she would have fallen through the ceiling. Then she went around the chimney and lifted the attic hatch from inside a closet, and lowered herself down to the carpet. Calmly she walked to the door and thanked the man with the truck. The lecture she gave us afterward worked, and we sat in time out for a long, long time.

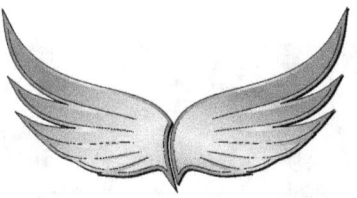

Chapter Five

We had a park in town, and I scared Mom bad one day. Brother and I visited the park once or twice a week. Mom made it fun for us three and sometimes she packed a picnic—usually chicken nuggets and honey. Mom always watched us carefully as we played, and she pushed us on the swings and the merry-go-round, and she climbed up the steps on the small slide with us. Gene was first, me second, and Mom was one step behind us. At the top of the slide was an area to stand—big enough for five or six kids, I think.

She always told us to stay away from the sides, as she was afraid we would fall. First Gene would go down, as he was bigger and had played on this slide a lot more than me. Then Mom would hold me in front of her and together we followed Brother. This was fun. One time, Mom had to help Gene with a scraped knee (from the sand) and she told me to wait for her before going up the steps of the slide. Of course, I took that brief moment to climb the steps fast! I was at the top near the side, waiting for Mom. I called her, and she turned around. Then, in slow motion, she was running to save me as I fell head

Gene and Sam 12 December 1987 ~ Gene's 4th Birthday

first onto the hard ground. She just knew I must have a broken neck or concussion. Before she reached me, I was standing up. She grabbed me and looked me over. Then she lifted me up into her arms, and Brother went with us to the doctor. I came out all right, not sure my Mom did though.

Mom loved to bake, and she always made us fancy cakes for our birthday. Neighbor kids and friends would come to the parties. At times, Gene would start talking about one of his friends, and then I would be jealous, so I would start talking about one of mine from preschool.

Chapter Five   19

12 December 1988 ~ Gene is 5, Sam will be 4 in April 1989

We could get loud from the sugar rush, and Mom always made it fun for us. She made sure that we ate our grilled cheese sandwiches first.

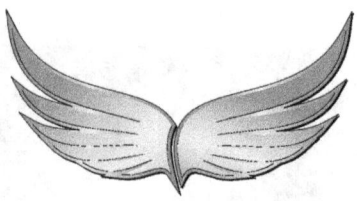

Chapter Six

I remember when Gene and I had our red backpacks, and how some mornings we would have to put them on before we got dressed. I loved my big brother a lot. We packed pencils and crayons and small cars into our packs—things to play with.

Gene and Sam with Backpacks

Gene and Sam Easter 1989

We also loved Easter because we liked the candy. Later on, I would learn of Jesus and Heaven, but when little we loved waking up to find our yard littered with wrapped candy. Mom knew Slim did this but she didn't tell us for a long, long time.

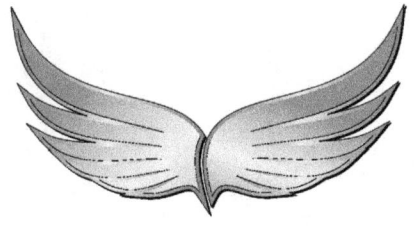

PART TWO:

Cancer Arrived

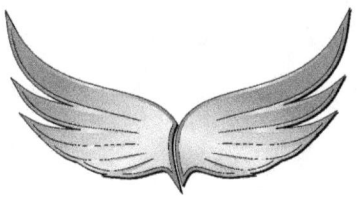

Chapter Seven

In June of 1989, the three of us moved to Ellsworth. This was nice because we went to school in this town and Mom worked in town. During this summer, Brother and I rode our bikes a lot and Mom always took us to the swimming pool. Sometimes she took us to the lake. Other times, she would take us to the parks, and there were three parks back then. We had a lot of fun.

In the fall, Mom started dating Michael. He was a really nice and funny guy. Did you know that he could talk like Donald Duck?

That same fall I was getting sick all the time. I had sinus infections, mononucleosis, inner and middle ear infections, and upper respiratory diseases. Gene was well and so was my Mom. I kept getting sick, so Mom took me to see a lot of doctors and pediatricians in an effort to find out why. She took me to see a lot of specialists—she did all she could every week with doctors. I was still able to attend preschool (part-time), and I loved seeing my friends there, and my teacher, Mrs. H.

Both Gene and I wore Pilgrim hats that Thanksgiving, the ones we made in kindergarten and preschool. I ate a lot of

Thanksgiving 1989 ~ Last One at Home with Mom and Family

food that day and didn't feel so good. I had a head hurt that just wouldn't go away, but the fun I had with my cousins was awesome. We had fun playing and tossing a football.

Come December, I was still having to take antibiotics. It was a vicious cycle of doctors and medicine. The same for January and more than twice in a week! CT scans (pictures like X-rays) of my head and neck were done. The X-ray doctor read my scans as normal for a child my age. We had no clue that the radiologist tragically misread the scan, and missed a tumor mass in my neck and head.

Mom took me to see another doctor who doctored ears, noses, and throats. Two days later, the doctor put tubes inside my ears. He had trouble getting the tube in my right ear to stay in place, and he didn't take the time to find out why this was so. My cancer tumor could have been found if he had only looked. On follow-up visits all I was given was another antibiotic. My head hurt. I had a Big Head Hurt! I never told Mom that my head hurt though.

Two weeks later, Mom was horrified to find the right side of my face drooping. The doctors could not tell her why this was, and she let them know that they better figure things out fast!

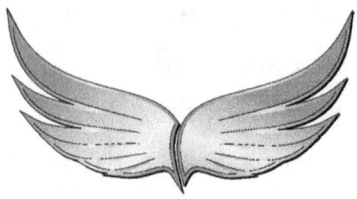

Chapter Eight

In early March 1990, Mom noticed that I had lost the peripheral vision in my right eye, and straight to the emergency room we went! They did another CT scan of my head and neck, and then the doctors told Mom I had a tumor mass the size of her fist in my neck and head. Mom signed surgery forms, I was taken in for a biopsy (a look at the tumor), and cancer was found. I had Rhabdomyosarcoma. That is a BIG word, I don't like that word, and it was scary to me.

While Mom was reading the CT scan result, I could tell she wasn't happy with the findings.

Michael called to see how I was, and he made sure Mom's car would get her and us to where we needed to be.

Mom and Brother stayed the night with me. Gene was just age six then, and Mom held Brother while she reached out to touch my hand and soothe me. We were in this together. We'd fight this.

Mom was figuring out which hospital I would be treated at, and she worried about the time she would be away from Gene. Mom went to both schools and explained the situation. Ardy was our babysitter, and Mom made plans with her to keep Gene while we had to go to the big city hospital, KUMC (University of Kansas Medical Center).

I had to ride in an ambulance with lights on the whole 230 miles and Mom drove behind us!

At KUMC we found out that my cancer couldn't be operated on. I was to have radiation and chemotherapy (medicine). The doctors ordered a lot of tests and my veins were poked many times. We did get to talk to Gene on the phone that evening. He liked kindergarten.

Over the next weeks and months, many things happened. I had a lot of pain at times, bad pain. I was crying, and my nurse, Rita, would give me morphine.

Two more spots of cancer were found in each lung. I had an IV pump and received IV morphine for pain and other medicines.

I decided to call my IV pump "Herman," as another boy with cancer called his pump Herman. I liked the sound of that name. Mom would put me in a wheelchair, grab Herman, and off for a walk we would go. KUMC was huge! I saw so many different places and two gift shops. I also got to see an escalator for the first time. One time I told Mom, "I think you're lost."

Mom said, "No, I'm not." She was right, as we did get back to my room. Mom stayed every night at my bedside.

Two weeks after starting cancer treatment, I suddenly burst out, "Mom, my head don't hurt no more." I touched my head and then I told her that my neck didn't hurt. Mom had tears running down her cheeks. Then I told her that sometimes, when I got up in the night and went to her bed, I was not scared, but I had a Big Head Hurt. She asked me why I didn't tell her about the hurt in my head, but I never answered her. I didn't want to.

One day I saw a little boy with no hair on his head, and I wondered if that would happen to me. My doctors came in, and I listened to them and Mom talking. I didn't understand chemo and radiation, but one doctor told me that I had little cancer ghosts (bad guys) in my body that made me sick. He said the chemo and radiation were the good guys, and that they would kill the bad guys so I would get well. *Ghostbusters* was one of my favorite movies to watch, so I imagined how the good guys would go after the bad cancer ghosts. Chemo was started, and I had two radiation treatments each day.

I hated the first time being on the cold table in radiation. My doctor had to fit me with a plaster mask of my head and neck. I was scared and crying. When they were done making marks on the plaster, the area for radiation was then completed. That mask scared me each time I had to wear it.

The next day I received a Hickman catheter in surgery, kind of like a big IV in my right chest. I was to receive medicine through it.

Mom helped me out with my cares every day. Mom was excited when the doctors said that no bad guys were found in my spinal fluid or bone marrow.

Mom seemed to pray a lot. I'm not sure who she was talking to, but I heard her pray and give thanks to God.

Radiation was hard on my little body, and I was tired and weak. I always got to take Precious, my stuffed bear, with me to radiation, and that helped. My preschool teacher, Mrs. H, had given me Precious to take to KUMC. Mom told me that they had to sedate me during my first two weeks of radiation. I didn't understand, so she explained that they put some sleepy medicine through my Hickman to keep me still.

I had trouble swallowing food, so they started me on TPN (Total Parenteral Nutrition) IV food through my Hickman every night.

For a long time, I threw up a lot with the chemo, and they tried to find a medicine to help me. Sometimes the medicine helped.

One day Mom had a surprise for Me—a Jayhawks baseball cap! Wow! I loved that baseball cap.

In the evenings, and if I was feeling okay, I would talk to Gene and Ardy on the phone. Mom did too, and she talked to Michael a lot. They prayed together on the phone every evening. I think I knew who she was praying to, but I had to make sure. I listened each time, as I was curious.

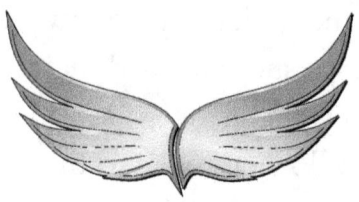

Chapter Nine

Mom learned how to change my Hickman dressing in a sterile way; the nurse watched her do this and was okay with it, so Mom did it every day after that first time. We would talk together every morning, and we talked of missing Gene. Mom was writing letters to people. I know she wrote some to Brother and Michael. Mom was happy when she would receive a letter back from Michael, and I was thinking he could be my new daddy. Mom wrote a lot every day. If a doctor was in the room and talking, there would be Mom writing in her book.

Mom and I explored the hospital on my good days, and on bad days we played in my room or she would chase down a VCR (videocassette recorder) so that I could watch *Ghostbusters*.

Mom did math every morning. I didn't know what math was, so I just listened. This is how Mom did her math: *Mom would get my lab report and calculate my ANC (absolute neutrophil count). The reason she did this was the absolute neutrophil count, the number of white blood cells (WBCs) that are neutrophils are obtained by multiplying the WBC count times the percent of neutrophils in the differential WBC count.* She was speaking Greek to me. Mom knew how to do this. I found out that when my ANC was low, I could not receive chemo or radiation, and I could catch a germ easily.

After a few weeks passed, we had a routine going each day. On our trips to radiation oncology we passed through the halls where many people greeted me by name!

One day Mom sneaked off while I was taking a nap. I was awake when she came back into my room carrying a huge plastic bag that had a Jayhawk on it. I insisted on looking inside, just a peek, and I looked. I smiled a Huge smile when I saw that it contained a KU basketball—a small one made of rubber. Mom told me it was for my birthday the next day, but I got

Sam Checking out the Flowers at KUMC Spring of 1990

it the day before my birthday. I played with it the rest of the day, and at bedtime I held it next to me while I slept.

By this time, when Mom took me to receive radiation, she was happy I could do the treatment without sedation. My stuffed bear, Precious, always lay next to me.

I started having trouble swallowing. Spit would build up in my mouth, so Mom used a Yankauer suction on me, but mostly I just used it myself to clean up my own extra spit—Mom called it 'oral secretions'. I felt like a Big Boy in doing this for myself.

One day I accidentally peed the bed while asleep during chemo. Mom gave me a bath, and she put an adult diaper on me. I raised a fit! Not for a five-year-old boy! Tomorrow I would be age five. No! I finally gave in and wore them. I was tired of the medicine, and we had been here for an entire month already.

Mom told me that Michael called her after I fell asleep and they talked for almost an hour.

The next morning, I remembered it was my birthday! April 6, 1990, was the day I turned five years old! I wished my brother, Gene, was here. I missed him a lot. Mom missed him, too. Mom told me "Happy Fifth Birthday" this morning. Then she took me down to receive radiation.

I was in for a Huge surprise when we arrived. My nurse, Vickie, had a birthday present for me, and the technicians had the radiation table decorated with balloons and toys. There was even a birthday banner. Mom took pictures of my surprise.

Upon arriving back to my room, my nurse, Rita, asked Mom to take me for a walk. Rita told us to come back in fifteen minutes. I wasn't sure how long fifteen minutes was, but I did know something was going to happen. Upon arriving back to my room, I yelled in glee! My room was decorated for my birthday, and there were birthday cards on the table. A remote control Cosmos car was beside the cards.

Then the nurses and other hospital staff sang "Happy Birthday" to me. I know I was smiling. That wasn't all! Dennis, the maintenance man who I liked, brought me an indoor Nerf basketball and hoop set. I got to have my fifth birthday party, but I was missing Gene. Mom called Ardy and we both got to talk with her and Brother.

In the afternoon, Mom took me back down for radiation, and I was surprised again! The receptionist gave me an Easter basket. Wow! It had turned out to be a great birthday, but I missed my brother. While sitting in my Mom's lap, I whispered to her, "I miss my brother." Mom was in tears that she tried to hide from me, but I could tell.

I started another round of chemo the next day. The sleepy medicine didn't work this time, and I was all over my bed and in a rage. Later that day, when I was back to being normal, Mom took me to the Easter party in the hospital. There were clowns at the party and they did tricks. I felt a little better as I watched the show.

Mom told me the party was sponsored by Dream Factory, an organization that grants a dream wish to each child going through cancer or any serious long-term illness. They wanted to grant me a wish. I told Mom that I would think about what I really wanted. After the Easter party, Mom mailed off a letter to Gene.

My red blood cell count (RBC) dropped low, and I was given packed red blood cells through my Hickman. I thought they looked funny in the tubing since they were red. After that,

Sam and Gene in April 1990 ~ First Time Together at KUMC

Mom took me down to one of the KUMC gift shops. I had birthday money to spend. I know I was smiling as I looked around the gift shop. I carefully selected two toys, and I got to pay for them myself with the money in my Batman wallet.

The next morning, Mom found my golden blonde hair all over my bed. I could tell she was crying and doing her best to hide it from me. I touched my head and knew I looked like the other kids on my hospital unit, but I never cried. I was going to be tough and hide my tears deep inside of me.

When Mom was done with cleaning me up, I received more chemo and packed red blood cells. My medicine didn't work, so I threw up a lot. Mom cleaned me up each time. Being a kid with cancer is hard work. I hated it but I knew the good guys were fighting the bad guys. I wanted the good guys to win!

I woke up in the middle of the night and asked Mom to lie down next to me. When she did, she laid her arm around me in a hug and told me she loved me dearly. Her hugs and words made me feel better.

I didn't feel good today, so Mom put a face mask on me, and then she took me outside so that I could ride my red Big Wheel. I had to wear a face mask so that I wouldn't get any germs.

After my nap, Mom filled up a water squirt gun for me. Then she placed a mask on me and I ran off to squirt water on the nurses. The nurses also squirted some water on me. Mom said this water fight lasted for about an hour.

Mom did her best to call Ardy around the same time each day so that I could talk with her and my brother, Gene. Of course, Mom talked to them also. I missed Brother. I missed being home. Mom called Michael after she thought I was asleep. She was crying but Michael always seemed to know the right things to say to her.

One day Mom came back from the nurses' desk and caught me trying to feed my goldfish some 7-up. I guess goldfish don't drink what we drink. My goldfish found a new home, and that was okay with me.

I did not want to be in the hospital any longer, and I wanted the doctor to give me all of the good guys all at once so I could go home. Instead, my ANC was too low for the good guys and my platelets (makes blood clot) was low, so I received platelets through my Hickman. The outside of my neck felt like it was on fire, so Mom put Aquaphor on my skin. My radiation treatment caused my skin to burn and hurt.

My right eye also hurt from the radiation, so Mom put drops in, and I wore an eye patch. I pretended that I was a pirate!

Then Mom told me that she had to leave the hospital and go home to check on Brother. I cried because I didn't want her to leave. Mom said she would bring Gene back with her. I wanted to see him, but I wanted Mom to stay here, as I was scared. We both cried as she left, but I knew she was coming back and that made me happy.

I woke up the next morning and saw my brother! I saw Gene sitting on the floor playing quietly. Immediately I yelled out, "Brother, Brother!"

I jumped out of bed and grabbed Gene in a Big bear hug. We played the rest of the day. I woke up and saw Gene the next morning. We played that day, too, until Michael and Karen arrived to take Gene back to Ellsworth.

Ardy called around bedtime, and Mom and I got to talk with Gene and Ardy.

Every day here in the hospital was the same. I wanted to go home. One afternoon, mom took me outside to get some sunshine. I rode around on my red Big Wheel all over the patio area that was next to the KUMC bookstore. Mom took pictures, and in one of them she caught me watering a flower with my squirt gun.

The very next day, I got to go to the school room on the unit. I liked my teacher, Kristy, and I painted a picture, which Mom taped on the wall of my room. By now, my wall was

Sam Squirting Gene's Play Watch at KUMC in April 1990

decorated with lots of birthday cards, and the calendar I placed stickers on after each radiation. I loved the stickers! I also had a lot of stuffed animals like bears, turtles, and fish.

The next day, I received another blood transfusion and Mom chased down a VCR so that I could watch *Superman*.

Every evening I got to talk to Gene and Ardy on the phone. While Mom thought I was asleep, I could hear her side of her call with Michael. I wondered if Michael would be my new daddy?

The next day I received more chemo, and Mom let me watch both *Ghostbusters* and *Batman* movies.

Right before I fell asleep, Michael called Mom. He asked her how I was doing, and asked if Mom needed anything. Then I heard Mom tell Michael, "I love you." He must have told Mom that he loved her, too, as she was crying and so happy.

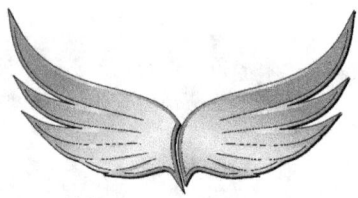

Chapter Ten

Today is my 59th day of being in the hospital. I just wanted my treatments done and over with. Mom was talking quietly with a nurse and I overheard that little Jill had passed away. I didn't know what "passed away" meant, but Mom and my nurse were sad. Something bad must have happened to her, but I didn't ask Mom. Jill was age three. I heard them say the word "Heaven," and I was curious. I kept this to myself, as I wanted to think about it.

In the afternoon, Gene arrived for a visit. I was glad to see him. We hugged and played and I gave Gene some of my stickers, as I wanted my brother to have some of his own. We talked non-stop. At bedtime, Gene had to leave for the night and sleep at the Ronald McDonald House. It was across the street from KUMC. The next day we played again and Gene showed me how to play Nintendo. We liked Mario. Then Gene had to go back home and I wanted to go with him, but that was not allowed. The doctor said I needed another blood transfusion and some platelets.

I overheard Mom talking with Michael on the phone before I fell asleep. They talked for a long time, and I heard them pray to God. As I fell asleep, I wondered who God was and why I could not see who they were talking to. It was just Mom and me in my room.

Days were pretty much the same when Gene wasn't here visiting. One night I woke up sick, sick, sick! This happened every time I received chemo. I could not stop vomiting and I asked Mom for a doctor. This was a big deal as I never asked for a doctor before, but now I needed one. My tummy hurt bad—a Huge Tummy Hurt. I received medicine to help my pain.

The next day I was tired after having a bad night, so I played lightly with Precious, my stuffed bear. When I would take a nap, Mom would take a nap. I just kept falling asleep to my favorite movies. That night a Huge thunderstorm passed over the Kansas City area. The next morning I was tired and so was Mom. When Mom took me down for my radiation treatment, everything was flooded. We saw one of the doctors sitting on a stool chair, in a foot of water, writing orders. I thought he looked funny with all the water and I laughed. Mom laughed too. I did not get to have radiation due to the flooding. We spent the day resting and playing in my hospital room.

The doctor came in to tell Mom that a biopsy (a tiny piece of tissue to look at) of my lung needed to be done. The surgery would not be done at this time though. They were talking about the good things, and the bad things that could happen during surgery. To do the biopsy, I would have open lung surgery. I was anxious and then I heard Mom praying for me to God. I decided it was time for me to get to know God! I never told Mom but I did start talking with the Lord and I learned about Heaven. I think Mom didn't tell me about Heaven because she was afraid that if she did, I would go there and she would be sad.

A few days later, I was having fevers and Mom and my nurse did what they could to get them down. Mom said I was at 101.3 F. Gene was here visiting and after I went to sleep, Mom took him down to the chapel in the Murphy building and they prayed for me. Mom told Gene everything she could about God and Heaven, and when I woke up she told me everything she had told Gene. I didn't tell her I had already talked with Jesus, but I did smile at Mom.

I woke up in the middle of the night a few days later. I was hungry and I wanted watermelon. I demanded watermelon. The patient refrigerator didn't have any and the kitchen didn't have any, so Mom told me she was going to find a store with watermelon and she did just that! I ate half of the watermelon Mom brought back to me. I had watermelon juice all over me and I was grinning. I was a happy little boy right then and my tummy was full.

Mom took me to the KUMC gift shop to spend more of my birthday money. I looked closely at everything and Mom told me no when I looked at a toy that cost more money than I had. I was choosy in what I bought, and I kept my birthday money in a Batman child's wallet.

The next morning I woke up hungry. I ate the rest of the watermelon and a little applesauce. Then I opened up a packet of mayonnaise and ate that too—just for the flavor! I always loved the taste of food. Mom just kept on smiling at me.

We watched movies and played with toys and had a quiet afternoon. In the evening we both got on the phone and talked with Gene and Ardy.

A couple days later, Mom wheeled me all over the KUMC hospital so I could see the entire building. A few areas we were not allowed to go inside of so we didn't.

A man from "Dream Factory" called again asking what my wish was and I couldn't decide if I wanted to have a pedal push "Batman Car" or if I wanted to go to Disney World in Florida and see my favorite Disney character, Donald Duck. Mom told me I had plenty of time to think about what I really wanted. I went to sleep right after we both spoke with Gene on the phone.

The days were mostly the same routine except for the days I was sedated or in isolation. This was my May of 1990. I have been here three months!

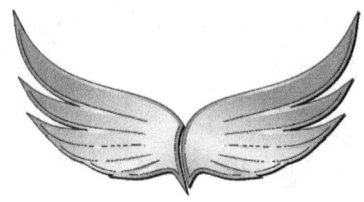

Chapter Eleven

I woke up in the middle of the night many times. Mom would always get me something to eat as I was hungry. Kids can get hungry sometimes while on chemo.

I hated having fevers and especially one that was 103.4 F. Mom or a nurse would give me liquid Tylenol. Sometimes, I would receive the Tylenol in my behind—the times when I couldn't swallow. I got better.

They did spinal taps (poking a needle through my lower back) often to check for cancer cells and to receive chemo. I never liked spinal taps and I cried.

One day Gene got sick. His fever was 101.6 F. Ardy took Gene to see the doctor for his cough, sore throat, headache, earache, and fever. The doctor gave Gene some medicine to take and I was happy about that.

Another day I heard Mom talking on the phone with Michael about my brother, Gene, his daughter, Rachel, and me. They talked about what they wanted for each of us, and what they wanted in life. I knew now that Michael would be my new daddy and I was happy about this. I wanted a nice daddy and

I knew I was grinning. I would have a new sister, too, and she would then be the baby in our family.

Each day was like the month of May with good days and bad days. One time I watched *Spider-Man* on the VCR and now I liked that movie, too. Some days were bad and I was sick and other days I felt better.

Mom took me to feed the frogs again—they were in the KUMC school teacher's classroom. That was a lot of fun. This was my last time to feed them as my teacher, Kristy, was taking them home for the summer. While there I painted a picture for Mom.

One morning I was really hungry, and I drank a full glass of apple juice and ate some Fruity Pebbles breakfast cereal, which was my favorite. Mom was making friends at the hospital. She made friends with other moms who had children with cancer. They would talk about the treatments the kids were receiving and sometimes I played with the younger kids. Mom also made friends with the parents of the kids who had other diseases. KUMC had a lot of kids who were sick and I didn't understand why so many kids were sick, and I wondered what God thought of this.

Total Pharmaceutical Care came in today to teach Mom how to use their IV Pump. They were talking about me going home! I was happy to hear that! Mom learned the pump and tubing fast. Then she learned how to add my medicine into a bag of TPN and rotate the bag until it was mixed. Mom did so much with my IV's every day and I knew she would do this for that company just like they wanted it done. I was proud of my Mom.

By this time my feet had grown. So Mom had to go out and buy me new tennis shoes and I was happy with my new shoes. They were awesome! I told Mom that I wanted my nurse, Rita, to come into my room and see my new shoes. They fit perfectly. Rita made a big deal out of them and I just smiled the entire time.

The month of June ended fast and I was so happy to have good days and evenings when I could talk on the phone with Gene and Ardy. Mom also talked to them and with Michael. I liked those evenings as they helped me feel like I was home—just a little bit—for just a few minutes.

Mom found out that I liked iced tea. She had gone to the nurses' desk to check on my labs, and when she came back into my room, I was drinking her iced tea. Mom laughed. June ended with me receiving chemo, and I watched *Cinderella*, *Ghostbusters*, and *Muppets Take Manhattan* on the VCR.

Goodbye June, and Hello July.

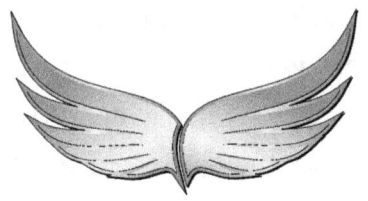

Chapter Twelve

I woke up early one morning, and I found Mom checking on my labs. I was to receive more packed red blood cells and probably platelets soon. Not every day at KUMC was good or bad. Some of them had both on the same day! How does that happen? My nurse gave me sleepy medicine so that I wouldn't react to my blood transfusion. As I fell asleep, I heard Mom on the phone talking with Michael. I was happy that they talked every single day. I know he prayed for me.

A few days later I woke up with my head hurting BAD! Mom called my nurse and I was given Tylenol, but I still had a Big Head Hurt. I begged Mom, "You gotta make me feel better." The doctor gave me strong medicine so my head no longer hurt as bad. The last time I had a headache this bad was back in March! I heard Mom praying for me as I fell asleep.

Gene came for a visit, but I was too sick to play, and I was sleepy. While the nurses watched me, Mom took Gene to Swope Park and the Kansas City Zoo. Mom told me she would take me there, too, when I got a little better. Gene had a fun time, and I was still asleep when they got back to my room. I also received platelets again. That evening Gene and I watched *Ghostbusters* on the VCR, and he lay next to me in my bed. Each day in the hospital was the same, yet different. I was getting tired of being here. I was scared the good guys were going to lose my battle with cancer.

Mom was sad the next morning, and I could tell she had been crying. She told me that today was Shane's birthday. My brother Shane had died eight years ago today and today was July 13th. We talked about Jesus and Heaven.

Sam at Home Riding his Red Bike for the Last Time...

The days started running together again, and I was tired of being here. I wanted to go home! My doctor said it was too early for me to go home. That evening, Mom and I spoke with Ardy and Gene. I told my brother I wanted to come home for a visit but the doctor had said no.

Seven days later I got to go HOME! I had been in the hospital for 140 days, and now my doctor said I could go home! I got to go home! I was grinning about going home. Mom loaded her car with my things and a nurse helped her.

By the time we got home, it was late and nighttime! Mom set up my IV stuff and got me on my TPN. She waited until I fell asleep before unloading the rest of our things from her car. Mom let Ardy know we were home and that we would pick up Gene in the morning.

After my sponge bath, Mom and I went over to Ardy's. I talked to everyone! I hugged Gene lots of times and then we finally left to go home. This was the first time the three of us had been together in Mom's car in 145 days. Mom always kept good records, and she always wrote notes on paper.

Gene and I started to play when we got home, and we were excited! A home health nurse stopped by and said everything looked good. When she left, Gene and I started talking about Teenage Mutant Ninja Turtles and my favorite one, Donatello. We were chatter bugs, and it was hard for Mom to get Gene and me to sleep, come bedtime. We talked about seeing Mickey Mouse and Donald Duck, as I had decided this was my wish— to go to Disney in Florida!

When I woke up the next morning, I couldn't believe where I was! I was home, and we had a great day. This was my second full day at home. Gene and I rode our red bikes with training wheels on our sidewalk. Mom smiled to see us so happy riding our bikes and being together.

I ate a few bites of chicken nuggets for dinner, and I was tired, and we all went to bed early.

On my third day at home, we went out to the country in the early evening and shot off a few fireworks. We just wanted to celebrate me being home and us being together, and we had a lot of fun.

On my fourth day at home, I had to go to the hospital to have lab work drawn. Mom wouldn't let the lab guy poke me, and so she asked for syringes and needles. Mom drew my labs from my Hickman like she did every morning at KUMC. The lab guy stared and I think he was surprised to see that it could be done. We lived in a small town of 2,500 people—Mom had told me this one time—and they don't see Hickman's placed in kids. Maybe, they never saw Hickman's at all!

It was a beautiful day, so we rode our bikes again. Joel of *The Ellsworth Reporter* newspaper stopped by for a story about me, and he also took a few photographs. He interviewed Mom and she told him about my cancer, my treatment, and what my wish was for Dream Factory. I also got to suck on a green popsicle.

Michael did some work on Mom's car so that it would be ready to head back to Kansas City. I didn't want to go back, but I knew I had to. Mom loaded her car, and then we left for the

Popsicle Time ~ Last Day at Home...

hospital after dropping Gene off at Ardy's. Goodbyes are hard to say and do. I cried. So did my Mom.

After we got to Kansas City, we went to the Ronald McDonald House. This was a Huge house with an elevator. It had three floors and a full basement. Mom got our room all fixed up with my supplies, and then we played Nintendo for a while. I was missing Gene, and I think Mom was, too. Food was brought in for the families staying at the house. There were TV's and games, and it was air-conditioned. I did play with the other kids at the house. It was fun.

When I got tired, Mom took me up to our room, and I fell asleep before she even got me hooked up to my TPN, as she told me the next morning.

Mom took me on a drive to see Kansas City the next day. I also went to KUMC for more lab work. Back at the Ronald McDonald House people shared root-beer floats with Will (another child with cancer—he had Rhabdomyosarcoma, too). It was his birthday, and he was be going home with his parents tomorrow. I couldn't eat my root-beer float.

Then Mom told me that we were going home again! We did just that and I got to spend two full days with Gene. I really loved those two days. Ardy called to check on me and Mom. Then she brought over Gene's red bike so we could ride bikes together, and we talked about everything, it seemed like. The visit was nice, and I loved being home.

When Mom took me back to Kansas City, I was admitted to room 5022. Mom looked worried to me. I don't think she liked the thought of me having surgery on my lung the next morning. Mom tried to explain to me what would happen the next morning, but I wasn't interested to hear it.

The next day, I wasn't allowed to drink anything, as I was going to have surgery on my lung. The plan was to do a biopsy on the one big spot in one lung. Mom still looked worried to me. I could just tell. Sometimes moms are not aware of kids picking up anxiety from them.

My nurses read my story in *The Ellsworth Reporter* that Joel wrote up. The staff loved the photo of me riding my red bike with training wheels. One nurse commented that they didn't see this side of the kids when they were at home.

Then we found out that THREE kids who had cancer got to go home with no more treatments! They won their cancer battles and we were happy for them!

In the early afternoon, Mom went with me and the staff down to the surgery area. I started asking her lots of questions about surgery. There was a nurse, Mom, and me in the room outside the operating room. I told Mom that I remembered they were going into my right lung and that I would be in ICU (Intensive Care Unit) after the surgery.

Then I asked my Mom a Big Question. I looked into her eyes and asked her, "Am I going to die?" Mom was stunned.

Sam Riding his Big Wheels Outside of KUMC

The nurse went quiet. Mom finally told me no—I wasn't going to die.

Then I asked, "Am I going to go to Heaven where Shane is?"

Mom finally told me, "Only if God really needs you right now."

"I want to go to Heaven, Mom," I said innocently. Then I repeated, "I want to go to Heaven, Mom."

It took a while, but Mom finally replied back. "We don't always get what we want in life. So you might have to stay with Mom for a while."

Mom didn't understand. I was tired of the pain and surgeries. She didn't know I talked to Jesus a lot. She didn't know what Heaven was like. But Jesus talked with me many times, and I knew Heaven was a wonderful place. I loved Jesus. Then they wheeled me into surgery.

After my surgery, the doctor told my Mom that they had removed the entire large tumor mass (it was Rhabdomyosarcoma), as well as some surrounding tissue. I listened to this talk that Mom and the doctor had, and I was in pain. Mom was allowed one hour with me in ICU, and I was in a lot of pain even with my nurse giving me morphine. Mom cried just like me. I had a drainage tube in my right lung and I was on a heart/respiration monitor as well. I had on a pediatric oxygen mist mask, and my nurse reminded Mom she could only stay for one hour with me. Mom didn't like that at all.

The second time Mom came into ICU, she got me to swallow some medications, but not all. Surgery was hard on a little kid like me. I did my best for Mom. Jesus was helping me.

The next time Mom came in to see me, both Mom and my nurse helped me stand up in my bed so I could pee! This was just five hours after surgery, but it had to be done. Mom stayed with me the rest of the night.

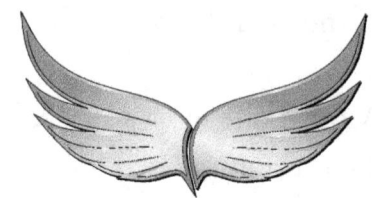

Chapter Thirteen

Mom checked on me all night long, and in the morning she gave me medicine and flushed my Hickman. My doctor removed the tube in my right lung, and I got to have some morphine, as it hurt!

Then they moved me back to 5D and the west step-down unit on 5D. I didn't need as much morphine then, but I still had a lot of pain.

I received a gift today—a real *He-Man* Power Sword. I was given the thirty-dollar kind that used batteries! I loved watching *He-Man* cartoons on TV just like I liked *Spider-Man*, *Batman*, and *Ghostbusters*. I couldn't really play with my new sword due to my pain from yesterday's surgery, but I kept it at my side. Sometimes I would turn on the button to light up the sword, even though I could not swing it around in play. Now I had my sword and Precious to sleep with me.

The next day, Mom finally got to hold me later in the morning. She carried me to my new room (5081) on the regular 5D unit, and I know she held me for at least an hour! Gene was allowed to be with me again and I was happy. I couldn't play just yet, but I loved having my brother with me.

Sam and Slim Tossing a Football...

I started to get stronger each day, and I even took eight steps before getting back in bed with help from Mom.

The following morning I was able to get out of bed by myself, so I walked over to a chair and sat down in it. Now I was down to one liter of oxygen per minute. In the afternoon, I got out of bed by myself again, and I walked on sixty squares of floor tile before I stopped. That was sixty feet, I walked! Then I had to have some morphine, as I was hurting.

Ten minutes later, I went for my next walk with Mom. I walked from my room by the 5F elevators through the 5D unit, and into the pediatric step-down unit. Then I turned around, and I walked back through all of 5D and all of 5F, up to the south-end window! After looking outside, I walked back through all of 5F and 5D to the 5D nurses' station, before returning to my room. That was a good three-hundred yards (Mom and my nurse told me this), so I was tired and ready to rest. Mom didn't know that Jesus was with us as we walked. Mom decided I was an amazing and brave little boy. She said that my brother Gene was amazing, too, since he was staying with Ardy most all the time, 230 miles away, and he couldn't be with Mom and me. I also got to stop being on oxygen.

I heard Mom and a nurse talking, and the nurse told Mom that little Dot died today—she had cancer. Mom told her that God had another angel child in Heaven. Mom didn't know this, but I already knew Dot was in Heaven because Jesus told me. We watched *Teenage Mutant Ninja Turtles* on TV before I went to sleep.

I got to go back to the Ronald McDonald House the next morning! Mom was happy for me and I was happy, too. I played *Mario Brothers* on the Nintendo with Gene before he left to go back to Ellsworth. Mom and I played outside the Ronald McDonald House today, and before we went back in, I planted one piece of a Sixlets candy in the sandbox. I told Mom, "I'm going to grow a bunch of candy." Mom just grinned at me. I remembered how Mom and Slim grew gardens.

I was receiving radiation treatments twice a day at KUMC. The radiation was on my lungs. I sure was sick to my stomach a lot each day. I hated being so sick. Medicine didn't work for me. After my afternoon treatment one day, Mom and I cuddled together on a sofa in the recreation room. We watched cartoons and napped.

Two days later, Mom and I were on the road back to Ellsworth! I got to be with my brother again! Ardy and Slim came to see me. I know I was grinning from ear to ear. Slim tossed a football with me, and Mom took some pictures. It was nice to be home for two days. Gene and I rode our red bikes again.

I knew we had to go back to the hospital on the third day, and we stayed at the Ronald McDonald House. After my morning radiation, Mom gave me a Big Surprise—we went to

Sam and Slim

Swope Park and the Kansas City Zoo! Mom put me in a zoo stroller since I wasn't strong enough to walk the zoo hills. I got to ride a Shetland pony with a real saddle, and I fed a giraffe. Have you ever fed a giraffe? Do you know how tall they are? It was a Big Zoo and I had a lot of fun with Mom.

After my morning radiation treatment the next day, I saw a Kansas City police car in the Ronald McDonald House parking lot. I started talking with Officer Ken Carson and his partner. Then I did a full inspection of the inside of their patrol car. That was fun! I wanted to push buttons, but they told me no.

We spent the evening playing with toys, doing puzzles, playing Nintendo, watching cartoons on TV, and talking about a zillion things—I was a chatterbox going on about the police car and buttons.

Mom took me over for my radiation treatments each time, and she always pushed me in a wheelchair. Did I tell you I have a kid's blue wheelchair? Mom told me that Cancer Action loaned it to us, back in May, to help me get to places too far to walk. My radiation table was in a different room and it was a different machine. My machine was broken, so they had me on the "Cobalt" table. I didn't know what that meant, but I was happy for the radiation and I had Precious with me. I felt better each day!

Mom called the grade school in Ellsworth and made arrangements for first grade for Gene and kindergarten for me. Then someone at the Ronald McDonald House asked Mom, "How do you do it each day with Sam so sick?" Mom became angry and told them that it wasn't like she or I had a choice in the matter.

Denise Vogue from Dream Factory called Mom, and she told them that the doctors would let them know when we could go to Orlando and Disney as soon as possible. I was excited to know we would fly on a Big Plane and see Mickey Mouse and Donald Duck. It was for the three of us, Mom, Gene, and me.

After I received my LAST radiation treatment one afternoon, Mom and I went home again! Gene and I played, but we didn't ride our bikes. It was evening time and we just wanted to be together. Mom did take us to the Dairy Queen for dinner, and then we went to bed not long after that. I could hear Mom on the phone, and I could tell that she was talking to Michael. They were talking about love, so I fell asleep knowing that Gene and I would have a new daddy.

That night I went to bed early, as I was tired, and Gene went to bed about an hour later. By accident, he woke me up as he got out of bed and went to Mom's room and her bed. I could hear Gene talking to Mom about me, death, and dying. I went back to sleep knowing Mom would answer his questions.

We had three days together at home and that was nice. Then we had to go back to KUMC. I didn't tell Mom that I was never going to be home with her and Gene again. But I knew I would go to Heaven, as Jesus had told me.

I was admitted to KU and all of a sudden my heart was beating too fast. So they kept me on a monitor and I received packed red blood cells, too. My heart went up as high as 170. No one could figure out why, except maybe my chemo caused heart damage.

The next day I stopped breathing for about 20 seconds. I kept doing this off and on, so Mom would shake my shoulder

Sam at Swope Park, Kansas City Zoo

and I would breathe again. My nurse watched me a lot, also. I knew all of this because Mom told me about it later on. Respiratory Therapy drew blood gas (arterial blood) from my wrist, I never felt the needle and I didn't wake up. I was taken to the PICU (Pediatric Intensive Care Unit), as I was not conscious. I stayed the same all day and all night the next night. Mom didn't know it, but I was with Jesus. Jesus was helping me by giving my body and my head a break from my cancer battle. I rested with Jesus as he told me about my Big Battle yet to come. The next morning I felt ready, and I just sort of "woke up" for Mom. Jesus had helped me back into my body and I just opened my eyes and blinked at the bright lights of PICU. I turned my head and looked at Mom. She was so happy! By noon I was off oxygen and back in my room on 5D. None of my doctors or nurses had any idea why this episode happened, but I knew. I had to rest with Jesus before my Big Battle. I didn't tell Mom about Jesus and my Big Battle, and I had Precious with me again.

A few days later I developed little blisters on my lips and around my mouth and chin. They hurt. Mom was sad that she couldn't kiss me with my blisters the way they were or she could get sick. I was also back in isolation again, so we watched TV and played when I was not resting or asleep.

TWO more kids went home today—FREE of cancer! Their Big Battles were over and the kids won!

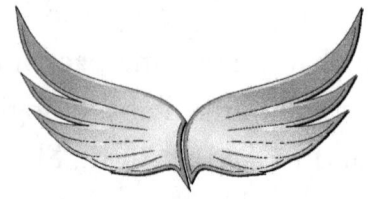

Chapter Fourteen

The doctors made their rounds of us kids this morning. My doctor said I had shingles and that I was contagious to other kids and adults.

I didn't like being in isolation again. Mom cuddled with me, and she was careful not to get germs from the shingles on herself or her hands. She wore a special gown and gloves. I loved the snuggles with Mom.

At night my oxygen levels dropped off and on, and I had to wear a pulse oximeter and oxygen mask. This happened every single night this month!

Visitors stopped by my room one day. Kristy Davis, my teacher at KUMC, brought me some kindergarten school work. Later a man from the Kansas City Royals baseball team came in with George Brett, and they gave me an autographed photo and an autographed baseball in a protective case. That was nice of them and Mom took some photos.

Mom would watch me write my name. My 'S' came out backwards but I didn't know it was backwards at the time. Then I wrote the letter A and it looked good. That M was kind of hard to write. First I drew one line down, then one line over,

Sam Laying on a Bear with a Bare Tummy

one down, one over, and one down. Mom was proud that I could now write my name and she made a big deal out of it.

Using crayons, I drew Mom two different drawings, and she taped them up on the wall of my hospital room. She told me that I was really good, and I just grinned—as big of a grin that I could do!

A clown from Ringling Brothers Barnum & Bailey Circus came to both 5D and 5F. I had to wear a mask for protection, but I had a great time with the clown. Mom took more photos.

One day I asked Mom if I could go back to Radiation Oncology. I told Mom that radiation killed off a lot of my cancer ghosts and that I wanted to kill more of them. Mom and my nurse, Lisa, told me that, for now, chemo and sleepy medicine would kill the cancer ghosts, and I said okay.

After my chemo finished this time, the plan was for me to go see Disney in Florida! Mom, Gene, and I would fly on a

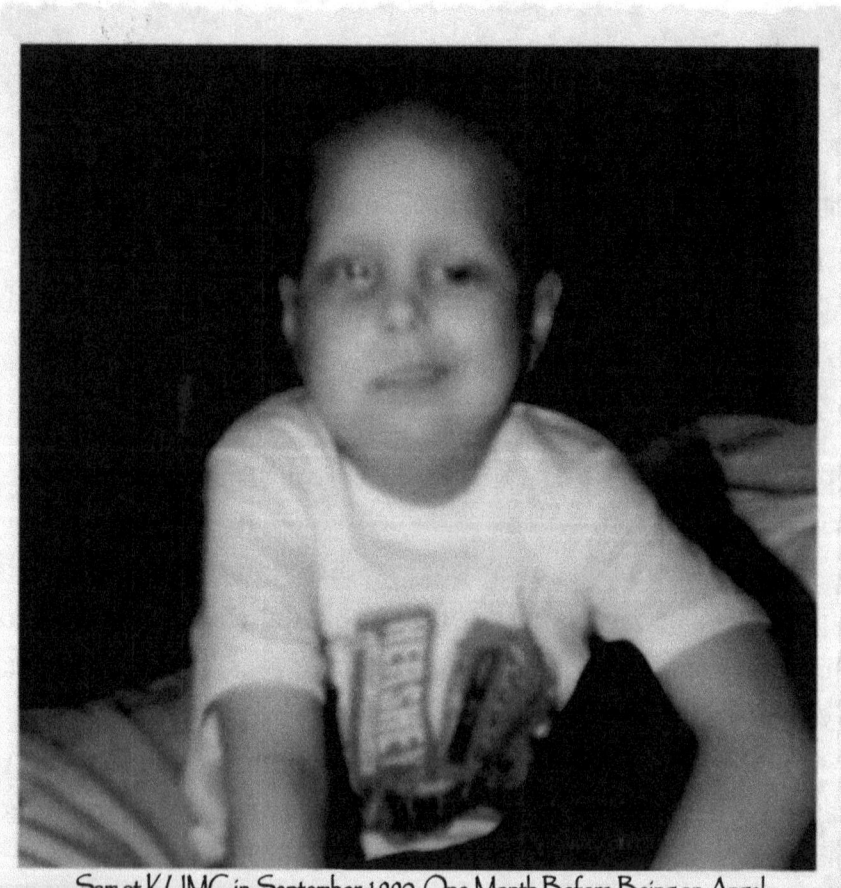

Sam at KUMC in September 1990, One Month Before Being an Angel

plane; and a child's wheelchair would be waiting for me when we landed. My TPN and other needs were already planned and set. I wanted to see Mickey Mouse and Donald Duck the most. Sadly, this didn't happen.

I was able to attend school in the hospital classroom on 5D. My teacher, Kristy, talked with my teacher in Ellsworth, and then she followed that plan for me. I got to have a picture taken of me laying on a stuffed bear with a bare belly for Mom. It was my teacher's idea. Mom loved that picture!

Sam in September of 1990 ~ KUMC

I was ready for school the next day! I planned to ride my red Captain Sam Big Wheel into the classroom. Mom told me that I couldn't, that some kids would only play with it and not do schoolwork, and I tried to argue but I finally said, "Okay, Mom. We will walk to the school," and so we did just that.

In the classroom, I was able to talk with other kids like me, and we did social activities. Mom peeked in a few times like the other parents did. Everyone loved the way Kristy did things in her classroom. She was just Great! She taught all ages! One girl I saw was missing a leg. I didn't ask her where it went, but Mom told me later that it had been removed as her cancer had spread. None of the kids had hair on their head. I liked going to school with other kids just like me.

Ardy called every evening. I got to speak with her and Gene, and so did Mom. The calls always made me feel better. Michael called every evening, as well.

After chemo one morning, I was wide awake and wanted to play Batman. Gene and I had talked about what we wanted to be dressed up as on Halloween. We planned to dress up as Ninja Turtles. Gene would dress as Michelangelo, and I would be Donatello. I had spoken of being Batman one time, and the nurses must have overheard me. They bought me a Batman costume! Mom helped me put it on, and then off I went as Batman with a fully loaded water squirt gun. I squirted water on anyone near me. It didn't matter if I knew them, I would just squirt, as I was Batman and no one knew it was really me.

I completely and totally broke Mom's heart today. I told her, "I'm sorry, Mom" and she asked me why. I repeated, "I'm sorry, Mom" and Mom asked again, "Why?" I finally said, "I'm sorry I want to go home." Mom told me we would as soon as the doctors said I could go. Mom didn't know that I wanted to go to my Heaven home with Jesus.

Father Spencer (KUMC priest) stopped by late one evening to check on me, and Mom prayed with him for me. Did you know he baptized me a couple of months ago? I liked being baptized.

Another day I needed lots of platelets badly. The one single donor in Kansas City wasn't able to donate that many to me. Mom prayed, she called all of the newspapers, and television and radio stations in an effort to get me more platelets. My body was letting blood leave me through my pee and when I threw up. I was weak, and I knew my Big Battle had started.

My doctor told Mom that between my chemo, radiation, gastric reflux, and my emesis (throw up stuff), my esophagus just couldn't heal.

When my isolation was lifted and I felt better, I rode my red Captain Sam Big Wheel in the hall.

Respiratory Therapy wanted to try me without oxygen one night and Mom said NO! They insisted that I was to have this test, and I had a BAD night. I threw up a lot, I had high fevers, and I did not sleep well. Mom didn't, either. Mom argued and begged them to stop the test, but they kept on doing it. I dropped to 30 percent on my oxygen saturation, and Mom finally ordered them out of my room! Then she grabbed an oxygen mask for me, she turned my oxygen back on, and I started to feel better. But the damage was done. I now had damage to my lungs and other areas of my body. The doctor told us later on that the test was to be done in the future and not last night. Mom cried and cried.

I Earned My Angel Wings

I was just starting my Big Battle. My fever shot up to 106.0 F! That is bad. My heart rate shot up to 225, my skin was partly blue, and Mom demanded PICU for me. When Dr. Landon came in, he said he wanted to try different medicines on me, and "see how it goes." Mom said, "PICU!" He wrote the order. Mom could really get the doctors to do what she wanted.

This was just how my September went for the most part. Lots of packed red cells and platelets. The pulse oximeter went off all the time when I was asleep. I was happy when isolation was lifted and I could be free again. I was sad every time I threw up or had fevers. I was sad to be back in PICU, and that my Big Battle had started.

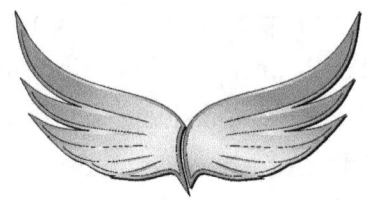

Chapter Fifteen

In PICU, I kept thrashing around in bed like crazy from oxygen depletion, and they had a special oxygen mask on me that forced me to breathe. But my lungs were too damaged. Finally, platelets were flown in for me from Wichita, and they were given to me in a Big syringe while my doctor tried to intubate me with a special breathing tube. It took him two times and I was terrified. Then I was hooked up to a ventilator (a breathing machine). We had to wait for platelets first or I would have bled to death and gone to Heaven. Mom stayed with me the whole time all of this was going on. Mom was with me when I was intubated.

My body was just eating up all of my packed red blood cells and platelets. My organs had been starved of oxygen for over ten hours yesterday. I was terrified and in pain. I knew I wouldn't win my Big Battle, and I also knew that I had to fight this battle because Jesus had told me so.

I received bunches of blood, platelets, antibiotics, and more for fifteen days. Mom gave me sponge baths, and she put ointment in my eyes. She talked with me all the time when I wasn't asleep. I cried each time I heard her voice. Tears flowed down my face.

They tried everything to save me. Mom was glad that Gene wasn't here to see me like this. Mom was happy she could talk to me, and caress my hands, arms, and face. I could feel her touch, but I couldn't move, as I had special medicine in me to stop me from moving (or I would have been pulling on my tubes).

Mom talked with my doctors, and they told her it was likely I would not live through my Big Battle. I already knew that, thanks to Jesus.

Mom liked to give me lots of mama kisses. I liked that. She prayed all the time.

I heard the PICU doctors talk about "shock damage" to my lungs. I had fifteen different tubes and wires. I know this, as Mom counted them and told me.

Mom told me that she spoke with Gene and Ardy. I was in the PICU so long that Mom had a routine she would do in caring for me. She washed my body, cleaned my ears and face, repositioned me, and she suctioned me through my breathing tube. She also made sure that my lips had a soothing balm on them, as they were dry and cracked. I got worse every day, no matter what the doctors tried to do.

Dr. Ardinger told Mom that we could try two things. One, I could stay on my current treatment until my heart gave out. Two, the medical staff could go in for a lung biopsy, and I could die on the table or a few hours later. It was decided to let me continue my Big Battle and no surgery. Mom also wanted me pain-free.

Mom spoke with Kristy Patterson, RN, with Dr. Landon and the KUMC social workers about my condition. She told them not to code me, and that she wanted an autopsy (getting body tissue and seeing what caused me to lose my Big Battle) done on me.

It was really impossible to ventilate lungs with that much lung tissue damage, and lungs don't heal. One day I opened my eyes and I saw MOM! I did this three different times and each time she told me, "I love you," and I nodded my head in agreement.

All of the 5D nurses took turns coming in to see me, as well as my teacher, Kristy. Father Spencer came in and prayed for me, and then he anointed my head with a special oil. Mom called me a trouper—tough to the finish!

On October 15, 1990, at 11:35 p.m. my heart stopped while Mom had her arms around me, as she held me the last fifteen minutes of my time on Earth. I was now in Heaven and with Jesus, and my Big Battle was over. Then Mom rocked my body in her arms for a good fifteen minutes.

The next morning Mom tried to tell my brother, Gene, that I was in Heaven, but he didn't understand what she was saying. Finally, he realized he would never see me again and they cried together.

At the funeral home in Ellsworth, I wore my Mickey Mouse T-shirt and jogging pants with white socks. Gene and Mom placed my KU Jayhawk cap in the casket with me. Then they added my favorite squirt gun in my right hand, and other things they placed around me: my "trick" calculator, my *Batman* play-suit, and my *He-Man* Power Sword at my right side.

They also placed my Donatello Ninja Turtle, my "witch" pin with moving eyes, a basket of M&M's, my packet of stickers, my autographed picture of George Brett along with my Kansas City Royals baseball, my stuffed Panda bear, Mickey Mouse and Donald Duck, and a colorful Snoopy Band-aid; plus Gene wanted me to have my "baby pillow," baby blanket, and stuffed Garfield. Precious was the last item to go inside with my little body.

Gene touched me and he also kissed my hand. Mom kissed me, too. Then my casket was sealed. My body was buried on October 18, 1990. It was a long and sad day for Gene and Mom. Staff from the 5D nursing unit at KUMC drove 230 miles for my service. I meant that much to the nursing staff!

The autopsy result came in and revealed that I was free of cancer. I HAD NO CANCER! I WON MY CANCER BATTLE! That is how I became a HERO at age FIVE!

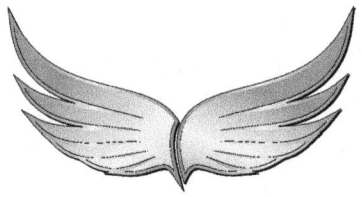

About the Authors

M. Schmidt is a retired registered nurse who won many awards in her career, a member of the Catholic Church, and has taught kindergarten Catechism. She has worked in various capacities for The American Cancer Society, March of Dimes, Cub and Boy Scouts, (son Gene is an Eagle Scout), and sponsored trips for high-school children's music. She loves all forms of art, but mostly focuses on the visual arts, such as amateur photography, traditional, and graphic art as her disabilities allow. More recently, she loves to devote precious time with her grandchildren and husband Michael. Contact her at ShaneGeneSamuel@gmail.com.

Gene D. Donley is a member of the Catholic Church, and has helped his Mom with The American Cancer Society and March of Dimes. He is an Eagle Scout who earned all of his badges working up the ladder through Cub and Boy Scouts.

Please leave a review.
Thank you.

Banners

M. Schmidt Productions
https://whenangelsfly.wordpress.com
ShaneGeneSamuel@gmail.com

Basic, Animated, & 3D Designs

eBook Cover Design

Fresh Ink Group
Independent Publisher

Fresh Ink Group
Push Pull Press

&

Hardcovers
Softcovers
All Ebook Platforms
Worldwide Distribution

&

Indie Author Services
Book Development, Editing, Proofing
Graphic/Cover Design
Video/Trailer Production
Website Creation
Social Media Management
Writing Contests
Writers' Blogs
Podcasts

&

Authors
Editors
Artists
Experts
Professionals

&

FreshInkGroup.com
Email: info@FreshInkGroup.com
Twitter: @FreshInkGroup
Google+: Fresh Ink Group
Facebook.com/FreshInkGroup
LinkedIn: Fresh Ink Group

Read the story of two little heroes and one mom

"I want to go to Heaven, Mom" he said innocently. Behind those blue eyes, I didn't see a speck of fear. And for a while I wondered where he got the concept of Heaven. I wanted to cry because I didn't want him to go just yet. Not now. Not in a few months. Certainly never before me, not if I could help it!

So I told him softly, "We don't always get what we want in life. So you might have to stay with Mom for a while." I knew not what to say next so we prayed together. I kept praying as Eli was given light sedation before surgery and they finally wheeled him away to the operating room at around 2 PM.

I lost my chance to ask Eli what he knew of Heaven. Why didn't I ask Eli? Why didn't I ask Eli what he knew of Jesus? Was I selfish to not want to give Eli back to God?

- Keepsake Hardcover
- Softcover Trade Edition
- All Ebooks, worldwide

Believe in Valentine Fairy Forests and tap into the flavor of a whimsical wedding and celebrate the love of two squirrels!

@MaryLSchmidt writes under the pen names S. Jackson and A. Raymond. She writes, Illustrates, and edits books for all ages. She believes that children should have books, and be read to, so children can explore their imaginations without limits.

Multi-award winner! Stop bullies, take a stand today and build up your child's image and self-esteem!

Teach children good touch/bad touch! Parents guide, ready to read with your child, teach the difference!

Mary L. Schmidt writes as S. Jackson and A. Raymond. She loves to write books for kids, especially those dealing with bullies and sexual molestation.

www.whenangelsfly.wordpress.com

www.ingramcontent.com/pod-product-compliance
Lightning Source LLC
Chambersburg PA
CBHW060104230426
43661CB00033B/1412/J